# PERIGEE

**WISCONSIN POETRY SERIES**

*Edited by Ronald Wallace and Sean Bishop*

# PERIGEE

## DIANE KERR

*The University of Wisconsin Press*

Publication of this book has been made possible, in part, through support from the Brittingham Trust.

The University of Wisconsin Press
728 State Street, Suite 443
Madison, Wisconsin 53706
uwpress.wisc.edu

Gray's Inn House, 127 Clerkenwell Road
London EC1R 5DB, United Kingdom
eurospanbookstore.com

Printed in the United States of America
This book may be available in a digital edition.

Library of Congress Cataloging-in-Publication Data

Names: Kerr, Diane, author.
Title: Perigee / Diane Kerr.
Other titles: Wisconsin poetry series.
Description: Madison, Wisconsin : The University of Wisconsin
            Press, [2020] | Series: Wisconsin poetry series
Identifiers: LCCN 2020016449 | ISBN 9780299330248 (paperback)
Subjects: LCGFT: Poetry.
Classification: LCC PS3611.E7634 P47 2020 | DDC 811/.6—dc23
LC record available at https://lccn.loc.gov/2020016449

FOR

*John S. McCall*

To whom do we tell what happened on Earth, for whom do we place huge mirrors in the hope that they will be filled up and will stay so?

   —CZESŁAW MIŁOSZ

To survive is an astonishing gift. The price of that gift is memory.

   —D. A. POWELL

# CONTENTS

## III. BLACK FOX

## IV. ZINC

# PERIGEE

# PROLOGUE

Open to the sky balcony-porch
off her upstairs corner room,
red tin floor, rusting, unsafe—
She wasn't allowed out there.

Winters the cold seeped under
the shut door stoppered
with a rolled-up scatter rug.
Ice glaze—couldn't go out there

on summer cricket nights either,
open screen door—stars, the moon!
Didn't matter, not allowed, unsafe,
didn't dare go out there.

She lay in bed, heart pounding as
around and around went the world
beyond the rickety railing—
no ladder, no rope, no going out there.

# I.

# *Timbered*

Not a woods anyone would want
to timber, new growth, scrubby,
you'd have to really look
for an oak big enough to take; still,
someone's hard at it, chain saw
whining, whining, then the pause,
the little silence after the completed slice,
the crackling crash,
the quiet thud.

It was like that—I could still move,
though I didn't know
I could still move.

Inside the skull cage began
years of battering to get out,
gray layers winding around
and around, tissue thin, accumulating,
solidifying, impossible to penetrate.

Years of relentless white dread
waiting for something to start,
waiting for something to end.

Let's see, if I was thirteen, then
it's our diamond anniversary.
Yes, 2016 less sixty, it was 1956
and you *were* fifty-six.

How I loved that you
were born with the century.
Afterward, it was always
easy to know
how old you are.

Were.   In the nineties,
my breathing eased.
Surely not, I said to myself,
no, surely he's not still

Which also means
you cannot tell, ever.
Wouldn't that make it
only mine, my secret?

Time to tell.   Hardest
of all substance, diamond
from the Greek *adamas*—diamond
meaning adamant, enduring

A filly for a filly
he must have figured.
Did he figure? Green-broke
three-year-old, just starting
to muscle up, no sense, easy
to spook, way too much horse
for a puny thirteen-year-old.
A quarter horse with quarter horse speed—
running away with me, bucking
dumping me off every chance she got—
why was this ok? I was his *best
little rider, best he ever taught,* he said,
but I wasn't.

Bay-colored, she was a copper bay.
White blaze shaped like a letter opener—
where did  get her?
She had a Spanish name
I didn't like, *Poco Mala Una,* wrong
translation for what should have been
*tu pequeño maldito,* "little bad one."
But she wasn't.

A thirteen-year-old wants
a name sweet, clear, a name
beautifully bay. At home
we had an apple orchard; I knew
about cider. I named her Cider.

Me, only me.

Not Nancy or Lynn or Bobbie
or Gerry or Gail.

Those small silly dancing ones
twirling in their crinoline skirts—
have you never noticed
the closed hand, the treat
slipped to them afterwards?

Jumping through flaming hoops,
riding the rump of a galloping
white horse, no dog enjoys
such stunts. Nor is it done by
coercion or threats.

Hunger's how it's done;
you only have to call once,
softly, to see who's hungry,
who comes trotting right over.

Did I say there's no threat?
Of course there's a threat,
choice, risk, possibility
of empty palm.

Early spring, April maybe, dusk,
no, more than dusk, almost dark, a gang
of neighbor kids, both of my brothers too,
play by the embankment to the hay mow.
He's given all of us
rides on his white donkeys,
but now the donkeys are safely
loaded into his decrepit horse trailer.
We don't want the fun to end—
the boys jump off the stone wall
like grasshoppers, then wrestle
on the damp ground. So early
the nights are still cold.
Now it's getting colder. I'm
thin, shivering; from behind
he puts his denim jacket around me,
his arms under the jacket—
warm, his man's body
solid and warm against me—
his hands stroking my arms
folded across my small belly; he's
talking, laughing, egging on the boys,
whom we can barely see now.
I'm wearing my first bra,
a training bra, training
my new breasts. Now
his hands move up under my tee shirt.
*A mistake,* I think, *he'll*
*stop, be embarrassed when*
*he realizes what he's doing, he'll*
*stop, pull away.*
It's completely dark now,
but it's the next second I need you
to see, the one when I know
it's not a mistake, when his fingers
first touch the little nipples,
that second and all that followed,
when I do not make a noise
or move or feel—when I disappear.

Gifts from me:

        Pencil and ink drawing
        of my horse
        Acrylic on cardboard painting
        of my horse
        Christmas cookies
        baked by my mother
        Brown leather gloves
        lined with white rabbit fur
        Unwitting prey
        Unwitting pleasure

Gifts from him:

        Mexican sombrero, real
        Cheap red cowboy hat, fake
        Pair of cowboy boots
        black, used, perfect fit
        Year's subscription
        to *Western Horseman*
        Rides on his white donkeys
        Rides on his Morgan stallion
        Lessons

Side step    side step    kick kick.
We are *The Little Pearls* though
my arm is still serving
its six-week sentence in a cast
from playing circus and falling
off a barrel backward.

Alas, in the special dark light
of dress rehearsal, my arm
in its fat plaster cocoon
shows up fluorescently—
a pearl with an appendage.

*Oh, dear me, no,* declares Miss Janus
and kicks me out of the recital.

Or tries to. My mother,
wrinkled housedress, snaggy stockings,
my two grubby brothers in tow, steps up:

*Not a remote chance, Lady.*
*We paid our fee, she gets to dance.*

And so I do.
                    I am the little pearl
at the end, the misshaped one
gamely bobbing and kicking away
in the dark with the rest of them.

My mother has done what she could do.

The boots? Yes, that's right,
used. No, never,
I never asked whose—
never occurred to me.

Black calfskin inlayed with white,
pattern of intertwined roses,
comfortable, already softened up.

Red-winged blackbirds swirling above
sunlit water spangling prancing hooves.
Morgan stallion, mahogany in motion
under the ecstatic girl, red Bermuda shorts,
red cowboy hat, white sleeveless blouse.
Back and forth across the shallow stream,
red and green mud turtles sliding off
warm rocks, cattails swaying by the banks.

Little picture, who kept you?
Who always knew
exactly where you were?

Little picture, who snapped you?
Who stood on the hill by the barn
just far enough back to capture you?

Even though the one I really wanted
was Skeeter, his Morgan stallion,
they were all agreed.

*Absolutely not!* said my mother,
eying the skittish stud prancing
and shaking his bridle.

*You heard your mother,* said my father.

And him, what did he say?
*Nah,* he smiled, *he's not for sale,
you just wait, I'll get you a good one.*

After I lead the beloved
into his box stall, after
I lay one stirrup up over
the seat and loosen
the cinch, after I lift the bulky
tooled saddle and Mexican
saddle blanket, hoist
both of them onto the rack
in the tack room, after
I unbuckle the ornate
bridle and slip the steel
snaffle out of his velvet
mouth, after I put on his halter,
wipe down his burgundy
withers and back, curry
him all over, after I unplait,
brush the long black mane
and tail, after I check
his water, his hay, give him
the oats with molasses he loves
for which he stamps
and whinnies impatiently,
after I go out and set the latch,
but before
                I can walk two stalls
down, before I can saddle up
my mare, before I can
put on my yellow leather cowgirl jacket
with the fringed sleeves, my hat,
my gloves, the red plaid wool scarf
to protect my face from the wind,
before I can slide open the heavy
wooden door, mount, and ride away,

he will get up from the bale of straw
where he sits watching me,
and it will begin.

The first time I saw the analyst,
of course, he wanted to know
all about my childhood.

*Idyllic,* I said, *lovely,* I said
*I was so lucky*
*to have been born in that place*
*at that time, before Milwaukee*
*swallowed up all the little villages.*
                    *We were free*
*to roam the woods, play*
*in the creeks, visit nearby farms.*
*My family had enough land*
*I could have my own horse.*

It must have taken my mother hours,
laying out the dismembered tissue
pattern of a cowgirl shirt, ghost
of what it would become—complicated,
pieced, set-in yoke scalloped
back and front, top-stitched facings,
inset sleeves, cuffs with pearl snaps
fastened to their grommets by a gadget
like a hole puncher.

And two-toned.
Sunflower brown and yellow, special
for the unsunny, unsmiling girl
who didn't like it or often wear it,
who left home as soon as she could,
who didn't take it with her,
or so she thought.

Once, he broke
the silence. He said,
*You're the coldest woman*
*I ever knew.*

*Woman,* I thought, *He thinks*
*I'm a woman.* Cold I didn't question;
I knew I was cold. No matter
how many layers I put on,
that whole year, bone-aching,
finger-burning, ear-ringing,
freezing cold.

He wasn't a Boston priest,
nor a New York, Pittsburgh,
Chicago, or Los Angeles one either.
He wasn't a Boy Scout leader or coach,
nor a father, grandfather, or uncle.

And he wasn't a teacher, no,
not even a riding teacher
unless you call watching a girl
ride around a barnyard and fall off
over and over teaching.

Horse trader, drifter, no account
ne'er-do-well, loser, he was
nothing, nobody. Then,
everything, everybody.

What I had to say on the occasion of Roy Moore's defeat:
*been waiting Roy been waiting sixty-two years for your*
*comeuppance small man your annulment null & voidance little*
*Roy your rejection election defeat as in Old French "desfait"—*
*undone as in now you've done become gone for doing those*
*little girls Roy the young stuff you liked that fourteen-year-old*
*one you would've liked me too me too huh Roy like you he had*
*a horse Roy a stallion bigger than your pinto Roy bigger than*
*yours way way bigger.*

When I asked him
about his family, he said,

*Old man kicked me out
when I was twelve.
Bummed around riding the rails
like a lot of guys were doing in those days,
learned to keep with the gandy dancers—
that's what they called them ones
who worked fixing the rails—
they looked out for me some.
Ended up going all the way to Frisco,
got with some bootleggers there.
That was in the twenties
when they had Prohibition and all.
They was rum-runners, went across
the bay at night in speedboats
with their lights off. Nah, never
got caught, too smart or too lucky—
hard to ever know which. I took up
working cattle after that,
found out I was real good
with horses—a natural everyone said.
Go home? Nah, never went back,
never saw any of them again,
nothing for me there,
never was.*

Mother's in the basement mangling
sheets smooth and white as paper.
Father, where is he? My brothers,
hiding in the woods, drinking father's beer.

Look, look, a man has taken me
to a horse show, look, look
what we've won! A trophy, look—
Best in Open Conformation.

Mother in the basement mangling,
my brothers passed out in the woods.
Father, where can he be?
Not home.

Look, I'm in the kitchen stealing
all the carrots for the winner.
Look, look at her little statue,
shining, golden.

Afterward, the long ride home.
Always it was deep winter,
always dusk, always snowing,
darkening blue cold biting
whatever wasn't covered—
my eyes, the thin space between
ankle and boot, glove and cuff.
He knew I could not be late, knew
they expected me at six for supper.

I knew he would let me go
by five. Snow deep in the fields
slowing my little mare, so bitter cold
I rode bareback. Between my legs
warmth radiated up as though
shame were seeping out,
freezing onto the outside of me,
turning to snow, always the snow, more
than half a century later, still coming down.

# II.

# *Blue Moon Suite*

Dawn in Jutland: gulls lift a flock of white commas
against a black page of newly plowed earth
as fog floats in from the Limfjord and lays
a milky cataract over quags and purpled heath—
time muffling memory of what happened where.

What is place but who was, or wasn't, there?
Upland, the fog slips across wheat-ripened fields,
past giant spools of straw strewn as if dropped,
as if the harvesters were called away, suddenly,
to another place written with their stories
or mine, my mother's, her mother's.

Near a byre, Guernseys in a pasture, their bags
full, lift their heads and listen for someone
in 1917, a milkmaid with my long arms, my eyes;
she comes softly, calling and calling.

My mother's poverty of no shoes not no new shoes no
shoes no safe house warm house with no rats dirt threats
hungry every day one lard sandwich every day in the lard
pail lunch pail walking to school in flour sack underpants
held up by inner-tube elastic poverty of great great big D
Depression poverty of little d depression under the radar
hidden depression the lonely no self self deprivation
poverty hungry self poverty unseen unrecognized =
unlovable not worth something some thing whatever
valuable wanted needed cherished as the special doll of the
never had a doll not privy to privilege of clean ironed sheets
no worms no dead mother no scarlet fever winter after
winter privilege of no worry worry leaking like the roof onto
everything everybody every body my mother's body my
body her biggest worry fear of frailty my frailty my asthma
eczema underweight high fever bleeder soft body sad heart
= softness = sadness sad soft body that would not harden o
little girl how will you ever survive?

My mother gave him his Danish name.
When he didn't come home the third day,
I started looking.
*Eepuss! Eepuss!* Not in the barn, the shed,
the chicken coop. He was a fighter,
sometimes stayed away a day or two,
hiding to recuperate.

Fourth day, I looked under the front porch.
I could see him way far back—his whiteness flat-looking.
*Eepuss! Eepuss!* I screamed, *Eepuss!* and ran
inside to get Mother. She grabbed an old towel
from the rag drawer, put her hands on my shoulders,
said, *I will get him for you,* then
crawled under the long porch across the dirt
through the cobwebs, got him.

She had on her pink begonias housedress,
my favorite.

*Once in a blue moon,* my mother says for times that don't happen very often. Sometimes, she takes me with to go shopping in Waukesha. If we go to Woolworth's, she gives me a quarter to spend on whatever I want. I go straight to the back to visit the goldfish and canaries. The little fish swim around in their bubbling glass houses that have divers and sunken pirate ships. The canaries sing in their cages, wooden floors creak under tall ceilings, big fans stir the dusty smelling air. In the toy department, bins of plastic dollhouse furniture—once I bought a tiny baby crib, another time a tiny baby with a white flannel diaper. All the regular dolls are lots more than a quarter, but I visit them anyway. One day there is a giant doll, big as a real two-year-old. She has curly blond hair, blue eyes that open and shut, white front teeth in her smiling mouth. I find my mother, take her hand, lead her back to see the treasure. *Oh please, can I have her, please can I?* My mother looks at me. *You have a lot of dolls.* Then she looks at the silent doll, her fat cheeks, perpetual smile. She looks at me again, *You really want her, don't you?* I nod enthusiastically. *Okay, little girl, okay, you get to have her.* She costs eight dollars.

Who's allowed me to go riding
in moonlight? My parents must be
gone to a Supervalu convention,
leaving my grandparents
in charge—I'm to eat dinner
at their house, sleep at mine.

Cider and I have come up to
the highest hill in the woods,
our lookout next to the shagbark
hickory, whose scattered shells
mean it's fall. The high yellow moon
is too small to be a supermoon,
too early to be the perigee.
So bright, I see clear across
the cornfield, past the new high school,
to my horse barn, our white house.

I know from geography class
why this woods is so hilly: it's
part of the *Kettle Moraine*
formed by a glacier which pushed itself
down this far, then stopped and receded,
leaving a *moraine*, all the ground-up
debris and boulders it had devoured, making
depressions—*kettles*—that became
ponds, lakes, and hillsides.

I'm crying and singing

> *Dark moon away up high up in the sky*
> *Oh tell me why oh tell me why*

I don't know why I'm crying or
what the "why" is I'm asking about.

Sitting on Cider at our moonlit lookout,
I have no understanding of what is forming
my geography, what will recede, leave
its debris, grow its woods.

*after Elizabeth Bishop*

It was nighttime and Father was driving (driving is a father job). We were up on one of those new *freeways* and we were going through a city and lights were everywhere—it was like the stars were on the ground! The streets had their own lights and almost all the houses had their lights on. I thought there are people in all those houses. Are there little girls and do they have Toni dolls who look like them and dogs and maybe brothers? Most of the windows had curtains so I couldn't see inside, but then one window didn't—I could see people sitting at a table! They were having supper—is it spaghetti and meatballs (my favorite) and why are they there and *them* and I'm here and *me*? Then the car went away from the no-curtains window, and I couldn't see it anymore. I could feel the car wheels rolling and rolling on the high-up freeway, and I could feel me riding and riding inside the car, and then we were out of the city and I could only see the dark. I could hear the motor rumbling and rumbling its one sound, and when I looked out the window and up in the sky, I could see the stars—the stars were all sparkling and sparkling and falling down and down and coming to the car window. Each star had a face I didn't know, and they were calling *come out here! come out here! what is your name? what is your name?* And then I was in the sky too flying all around with the stars. I said *I am Diane! I am the girl Diane!* Then I was back in our car and Father turned it into our driveway and we were home at our white and green house.

Blue moon—
air junk, smoke,
ash from fires and eruptions
and their messed-up particles
with wavelengths wider than
they should be

make a blue veil
a bogus template
for the moon viewer. Eye

of the beholder,
reader, eye of the beholder.

       That other label, *Betrayer Moon*,
who's the real betrayer?
Call culture,
call the Catholic Church and its
Gregorian calendar betrayer,
call cooking the books to protect
the so-called *Lenten Moon*
the betrayer.

Moon of extra,
moon of too early,
odd ball, unsuspecting,
innocent, out of place
blue moon.

When Christine Blasey Ford
testifies before Congress, I can't see
the middle-aged professional woman—
I'm listening to the radio—hear only
a terrified teenager whisper she's afraid
he will accidentally kill her, she can't
breathe, he's got her pinned to the bed,
he's grinding and grinding, then

I'm pinned to the ground,
the full weight of a man on me.
Beyond his head, pieces
of summer blue sky, small clouds.

Cider is tied in an abandoned
barn at the bottom of the hill.
He's said
he wants to teach me
how to drive, and I've driven
the dirt path up to the hilltop,
barely managing the pedals and shift.
We park, get out.

Below, I see Beaver and Pine lakes,
white cottages along their shorelines—
miniature houses in an electric train scene.

We're in the middle of a field of timothy
blowing in green waves. Suddenly,
he's playful,
teasing, tickling, chasing me,
play-wrestling, catching me,
letting me go, puts me in a headlock,
pushes me to the ground, rolls himself
on top of me.

He's not laughing or smiling now.
His gray-blue eyes stare, looking away.
He's grinding and grinding; I'm
gasping for air; I'm pinned.

It's his old car
that rescues me
as it starts to roll down the hill—
I haven't set the emergency brake—
he jumps up, runs to save it.

When he comes back,
he rolls his eyes, shakes his head,
tells me I'm hopeless, drives me
down to the barn.

I get Cider, ride home.

# III.

# *Black Fox*

The second time I saw the analyst,
I knew he couldn't really
read my mind, but I suspected
he was onto me.

I made sure I buttoned
the top button of my blouse.
Nothing slutty.

He was leaning back in his black leather
analyst chair, smiling, *Where were we?*

*I think I was sexually abused*
*when I was thirteen.*

He sat up,
picked up his notebook.

*Tell me exactly what happened.*

I told him.

*How long did it go on?*

I told him.

*Well, you were a little young for such pleasure.*

*Pleasure?*

*Yes, of course, you enjoyed it at some level.*

Then he swiveled in his chair to turn off
the phone buzzing behind him, but when
he turned back around—

there you were in your green and brown flannel shirt,
your silver belt buckle with the bucking bronco.

I could smell the hay, hear the horses breathing.

The good child,
I fed the dog, made my bed
without being told to,
brought home good
grades, teachers always said,
*She's quiet, no trouble, good.*

I was doing homework
in my brown and yellow room
that I loved, that she had made for me,
when she came in, face mottled,
teeth clenched, all of her trembling.

*I want to talk to you.*

The *you* in my ears—
tin foil against my metal fillings
if I accidentally got some in my mouth.

*I just got a phone call from that farm wife*
*where you go to those riding lessons.*
*Do you know what your teacher has been doing?*

She spat out the word *teacher* as if
she had bitten into a wormy apple.
I shook my head no, no.

*Don't you lie to me!* she hissed,
*He's been touching those tiny little girls out there.*
*Now you tell me, and don't you lie to me,*
*just what are you two up to out there?*
*Have you been fooling around with him?*

I shook my head no, no.

*You better be telling me the truth, young lady.*
*You keep messing around with him*
*you'll get yourself pregnant,*
*that's what you'll get!*

The good child, I did not lie.
I shook my head. *No, no,* I said.

Nobody else home.

      I am lying downstairs
      on the new gray sectional, what if

                      what if—could it happen
   by

           just by   could you?

      Every month, she told me
      I'd bleed every month.

        Not this month.    Not yet,

               not yet   not yet   what if
  who to ask
        who to ask?

When Uncle Jim got boils on his back,
my mother laid him carefully
face down on her white-sheeted bed.
Then, she washed the tiny volcanoes
with warm water and antiseptic,
held the miniature sword
of a new needle to candle flame
until it glowed red as hellfire.
With a quick and tiny prick,
she lanced them one by one.

They spurted up little fountains
clear as tears, then yellow pus
which she said was the poison.
So carefully, she covered every
little wound with gauze and tape.
I stood in the doorway, watching.

After TB took her mother,
a few years in the orphanage,
a few years with the hated stepmother,
my mother sewed her first curtains at twelve.

*Nothing to it, just straight seams.*
*Figured it out on my own*
*first place I was put out to work.*

Five dollars a week and board.
Laundry, cleaning, baby tending.
She knew to stay out of the barns
away from the hired hands.

*One came up behind me*
*out on the porch where I slept,*
*put his arms around me.*
*That was it. Left the next day,*
*moved on to the next place.*
*They weren't family, mind,*
*none of them, but I learned*
*everything I ever needed to know.*

So, the farmer's wife called my mother.
Nobody called the police.
No one did in those days.
They were too busy

      keeping quiet, containing the disgrace,
scandal, damage to the reputations
of my parents, of the little farm girls' parents,
of the little farm girls,
and me.

I tied the revelation about those little farm girls
to a cement hitching post in my mind,
didn't feed or water it for days at a time.

Glossary

Pedophile:
The most democratic. Lover
of all children, from the Greek
*pais*, child, and *philia*, love/
friendship, though
it's not love or friendship.

Nepiophilia:
Also known as Infantophilia—
toddlers or younger—
those tiny farm girls—
an offense which the DSM-IV
considers a disorder, unlike

Ephebophilia
As tricky to say as define
(consent, statutory rape, etc.)
from the Greek *ephebos*,
post-pubescent, or pubescent,
arrived at, or just arriving, like me

Neotonous:
From the Greeks again,
*neos*, young, and *teinen*, held onto,
youth extended, as in breast buds,
soft new grass pubic hair, slightest
curve to thigh and bottom, prompting

Lolicon:          Short for Lolita Syndrome,
                  in Japan the *manga* rage, comic book
                  porn of sexy eleven-year-olds,
                  wide-eyed, sucking on red popsicles.
                  Alas, all derived from great Nabokov's

Nymphet:          Well, really Humbert's term for, fantasy of
                  Lolita, who was really Delores,
                  who was, Nabokov once confided,
                  inspired by a little newspaper article
                  about a very special ape at the

*Jardin des Plantes*:  The Paris Zoo where
                  she had been carefully coaxed
                  into drawing with charcoal,
                  though all she ever produced
                  were the bars of her cage.

He wasn't all that tall.
He wasn't fast the way a horse,
a thoroughbred or quarter horse,
is fast, and he wasn't so strong
the way a pair of Belgians,
flax manes and tails swaying,
are really strong. I didn't know
how much he weighed,
but he had done farm labor
most of his life, with his hands—
his hands were definitely
the strongest part of him.
I weighed ninety-five pounds.
I knew just enough not to cross him,
not to tell, and to make sure he didn't tell,
not to not come back.

Third prize for my biggest "hand" one,
nearly all of them hands—grasping
gnarled hands, clawing fingers,
wormlike or scratchy twigs.
Old, all of them old hands.
The non-hand drawings are heads,
bowed fallen angel heads,
smeary blurs for halos.

Drawings so blatantly big,
they're hung high on the gym wall
for the Milwaukee Regional
High School Art Competition.
Ink and pastels, but not pastel colored.
Instead, lurid orange and purple-green,
old bruise yellow-brown.

One weird loner of nothing—
smaller, 8 by 10 blackness
surrounding a whirling red
bottomless hole—*Descent
into Hell* I'll title it years later
when I discover them
in my mother's attic
heaped in a pile, covered
with black plastic tucked
under each side so not a speck
of dirt could get in.

The same two dull wool skirts,
white long-sleeved blouses,
one pair of black shoes,
one pair of brown.

*Don't you want to go shopping? Why*
*don't you call up Nancy and get her*
*to go shopping with you in Milwaukee?*

Hair cut short as you can get it cut.
No jewelry, no makeup, no bright
red polish for the fingernails—
stubby, broken, dirty.

Seems a little weird to the others,
bookish, yet well-liked, everybody's friend,
though never anybody's girlfriend.

Bareback, I have given her her head
between the rows of new-mown alfalfa
in the back meadow where she is full-out
in three strides—so fast and low
I could reach down and touch
the fallen clover. We are heedless,
my eyes closed; again and again
and again we do this. I am never sorry
to remember how I crouched, my face
against her warm out-stretched neck,
how I whispered, *Yes! Yes! Go! Go!*

Math class, no matter how she tries,
she can't make sense of it.
There are rules; that much she knows,
absolute rules, immutable, rigid
numbers standing fixed, unforgiving,
unlike words, which she loves, which bend,
change, soften into different meaning,
equation, result.

Again she tries, retraces her steps
in the unyielding problem—back,
back she searches; if she had
done this differently, that differently,
done it the right way, the mistake
would not have happened, over
and over she tries to find the answer,
what she did wrong, how she failed.

My father reclines
in his green vinyl recliner,
having a beer, a cigarette.
He is really handsome.

I'm standing in the next room,
the dining room—doing what?
He calls to me,
*Are you happy?*

Startled, I hesitate.
*Sure, sure, I'm happy.*

He has beautiful black curly hair.
He works very, very hard.
He runs his own business.

*Your mother says*
*you're still going to see*
*that cowboy. Somebody*
*saw you riding out there.*

Busted, kids would say now.

*You have to stop it.*

*Ok, I will.*

*Ok, good girl.*

That was all.
He did not get up, did not
come into the dining room,
put his arm around me.
If you find that appalling,
you're wrong. It was enough.

The last time, I was walking home.
Warm sidewalk, lilacs, peonies,
Mrs. Ralph's long hedge of bridal wreath
all in bloom. His dark blue
Chevy drove up behind me,
slowing down when he spotted me.
From the rolled down window, he yelled,
*Where've you been?*

I shook my head. I did not
look at him, did not slow down.
I looked at the cement squares, their
predictable cracks one after another
past the Biermans' house, the Nelsons' house,
everyone inside or not home.

*What's the matter with you?* he called
hardly raising his voice.

I shook my head, and then we
went on like that, silent as in the old way,
except for the mumble of his car motor.
No other cars in either direction.
I did not look at him.

*Well, to hell with you!* he shouted
and tore away. Ahead,
I could see him roar past our house.

Someone's planted perennials along Ohio 71.
Deep blue delphinium wave in the wake of semis,
and to beautify middle America's median,
lace-feathered greenery of cosmos
balances bright and useless pinks and purples.

*If you can't eat it, don't plant it,* my mother said,
and for Grandma's roses she had the same scorn
she smeared on the sweet spikes
of white-belled lily of the valley
Grandma taught me to pick, one at a time,
bending over, pulling up the whole tender shoot.

I loved lilacs.
*Get those stinking lilacs out of this house!*
my mother said, *you know I'm allergic to lilacs!*

And she was. Always there was a throbbing headache
if there were lilacs. There were only lilacs
when her mother lay in the front parlor,
big chunks of ice in zinc tubs beneath the coffin.

Afterwards, came the Great Depression.
*Leftsa* for breakfast, lard sandwich in the lunch pail,
the long walk to the school by Nail Creek,
chicory eyes always hungry.

Tess's long tale of love
betrayed, over and over I read it.
No pregnancy, but the same
secret, as my sorrow also grew,
grew like an infant within me.
Like Tess I didn't want to read
other stories, didn't want
to know what had happened to me
was *just like thousands' and thousands',*
or that my *coming life and doings 'll*
*be like thousands' and thousands'.*

I loved the flamboyant bloody ending,
knew Hardy would have to kill her off,
knew *The President of the Immortals*
was done *sporting* with her.
I wasn't so sure he was done with me.

What I would tell me, the girl playing circus with her horse: You've somehow got Cider to stand still long enough for you to come running, grab a handful of mane, fling yourself up and on bareback—your "Flying Mount." That's allowed. You've scrounged two wooden pallets, stacked one on the other for her to get all four hooves on—it's taken weeks— but she's up. That's okay too, though this is not the circus— that horse is a quarter horse meant for cutting cattle and barrel racing. When you start standing on her, and I know full well your plan is a gallop around the pasture, I'll tolerate even that. It's when the phony ringmaster, whom I also know will show up in three more years, struts his black-booted red-coated strut into the ring, I will step up. I will hand you down safe behind me, grab the end of his black whip, thread myself hand over hand right up in his face, tell him: *This is not the circus. You are not the next one. Leave her the hell alone.*

I take it back—
there *was* an infant,
pink scrawny runt,
a sow's reject. How amused
he was to give her to me.
And my mother, not amused
when I brought her home.

*In February? She's too small.*
*She won't survive in that cold*
*horse barn of yours.*

She carried her inside, laid her
in a straw-filled box by the stove,
showed me how to fix the bottle,
feed her.

Squealing, squirting, rubbing
her hindquarters on the gate post—
"in season," they call it. The wild
dapple gray Arabian stud, his rush
to mount her, long teeth bared,
biting down on her neck, grunting,
her eyes rolled back, her scream
when he went into her.

Eleven months gestation,
the same year the inner fists
grip harder every month
in the relentless cramps
trying to wring me dry. I try too,
doubled over, bearing down
as if evil could be expelled, thinking,
*You've got this coming to you,*
*only right, only right.*

It was more wishing
for the unlikely—I never
tried to kill myself—
it was wishing,
the way a poor child might wish
for something she hasn't got
the proverbial snowball's chance
of getting for Christmas.

My family wasn't poor,
and they loved Christmas.
When I was in my chicken phase,
I got a rooster in a crate wrapped up
and red ribboned with a bow
under the tree in the family room—
big Rhode Island Red, iridescent tail;
he crowed through Christmas dinner.

      No, only wishing, hoping
for a car accident, a fire, cancer.
The crying was under control:
safely alone, cry, not alone, don't cry.

I never believed in an afterlife,
had always had a menagerie,
had buried a lot of animals.
At thirteen, cynicism grew,
spread its invisible rash
over all of me.

*What a friend we have in Jesus,*
we Lutherans warbled Sunday after Sunday.
*Is there trouble anywhere?*
*What a friend we have in Jesus,*
everybody's buddy up there
waiting for you with open arms.

*God no,* I thought,
*not another one.*

At the Oakwood Stables Horse Show
we waited together in the holding barn
for my event to begin. Some smart-alecky
stable boys pointed at me, started razzing him.

*Oh, whatcha got there mister? Pretty*
*little filly 'bout ready for breakin, huh?*
*Want us to get a saddle on her, get her*
*to throw you nice little stud colt? Huh?*

*What the hell's the matter with you guys?*
he shouted and got me out of there. I know
I am remembering that right—that is what he said,
and that is what he did.

It will throw them all off, so
yes to the safe boy, his moon-cratered
acne face, foreign exchange student
from Hamburg where in high school
they don't date; he will not
so much as try to hold my hand.

Yes also to learning to dance
the box-step in two awkward lessons
from Mr. Davis the history teacher.
Yes to the shopping trip
with Mother—see how happy
she is? Yes to the royal blue
disguise, the princess style dress. Perfect.
Yes to the giant chrysanthemum,
white with its red-letter A monogram—
Arrowhead High—homecoming, yes, perfect.

See, see everyone: normal.

October sliding into November,
rain and more rain, as it was
that fall I turned fifteen, clueless,
crying and crying as I rode
through the sodden woods, out of sight
though he was long gone by then.

No, no, he was there.
We were riding double;
he was there, up behind me, of course—
always from behind.

The girl I read about
in the paper this morning
didn't have a horse—she had
an ATV, which they found,
unlike her, pretty quickly.

She was horse-crazy too,
and that ATV got her out there
in no time—the guy
had a whole stable full.

A black fox sometimes followed me,
winters when I was out riding.
When it snows heavily, again I see him
thin and bold at the edge of the field, not hiding,

unimpressed by my trotting little mutt, Tinker—
a dog unique because she could come flying
and leap saddle-high for me to catch her.

This happened if it got too cold or the fox cried.
Then I put Tinker under my jacket. Her bristly fur

lay down safe against me, as if I held my own soul.
I rode carefully, mindful of my young mare in foal
and looked across the blowing field at hungry wildness,
at the fox still following, dragging in the darkness.

# IV.

## Zinc

And then what?
Marriage, children, yes.
And work, that too.
Haunted, not crippled.
The steel stake
the dog is chained to
leans, an inch one way
or another, but only if the dog
is exuberant, or furious,
leaps up, or lunges.

The dog's little world
packs down hard unless
it rains, and sometimes
it does rain.

Think of it as the penny
a foolish puppy swallows
that lodges in the pup's gut.
It's the zinc in the penny
that eats away, slowly,
unseen, unknown to anyone,
least of all the pup.

Rachel at thirteen, granddaughter
of eye shadow "Blueberry Passion" blue.
Rachel looks out upon the world,
says *whatever* and *like* a lot,
reads mysteries, has a boyfriend,
thinks about kissing, kissing him
a lot. A lepidopterist, her room

is all about butterflies, her favorite
*Danaus plexippus*, the common monarch
for whom she plants milkweed,
collects only those already dead
or too injured to migrate. The small
of Rachel's back curves like a calla lily.

If someone were to harm her,
as I was harmed, I would be able
to explode that person's head
like a dropped melon, with ax
or shotgun, calmly, surely.

That's what it means to be harmed—
calmly, surely. I believe this.

am I riding toward
or away from him
late afternoon the light
beginning to fail
black silhouetted against the sun
my mare and I gallop across the meadow
her mane and tail my ponytail flying
I'm lucky
though I do not know it
not because the horse
won't stumble in a groundhog hole
not because I won't get bucked off
nor even because I won't get
so much as a disease
let alone pregnant
at thirteen
I'll be seventy before
I allow myself to remember
the knives    guns
in the trunk of his car warning me
ride away    warning me
ride back toward
god how I loved that horse
who risked me
and saved me risked me
saved me

Not many people know my dog is a horse. One crisis after another with my mother now, many phone calls. *What did you do with my good quilt—did you steal it? What's the name of that new doctor, the one I don't like? I'm canceling that appointment. I kicked out that woman you hired, and she better not come back.* Usually, the day after I call her, she calls me—*Well, six weeks and you still haven't called your mother.* I drive the trek from Pittsburgh to Milwaukee often, and I always take my little horse with me. He settles in on his blanketed back seat, sleeping, hooves in the air, more comfortable than an Arabian stud in his mahogany box stall in Dubai. When we stop at rest stops, I put his halter on him, lead him to the grassy area. Children come running. They say, *Can we pet your dog? He's so big! Is he a golden retriever?* I say, *Sure, you can.* They don't know he's a horse, a small one. His name is Little Palomino. He stands there, accepting the adoration as if he were some kind of dog, a well-trained show dog winning his thousandth blue ribbon. When it's time to get going, I say, *C'mon, Little Palomino, time to go. Someone is waiting for us.*

My mother tells me
her earliest memory:

*I called and called to her.*
*Where was everyone? Where*
*was Dad? The baby upstairs*
*asleep probably, where was Thomas,*
*Alvina? Dad must have been*
*cultivating corn, or planting—*
*what season was it? Worn-out farmer*
*following a worn-out horse, row*
*after row—the miles that man walked.*
*Everything took more time, everything*
*done by hand. She was mixing bread;*
*there was a blue bowl. She was sitting*
*in a straight-backed chair by the window.*
*Forty-two, imagine. I was five.*
*She crumpled to the floor quiet—*
*a rag somebody dropped—*
*there wasn't a sound in that house.*
*Where in the world was everyone?*
*I called and called. Wake up!*
*Wake up, Mama! Wake up!*
*A blue bowl, dough stuck on the pieces, blue*
*like the middle one of my old mixing bowls,*
*you know, those ones I got years ago*
*from that deal the IGA had, the blue one.*

When the newborn
giraffe on YouTube
first tries to stand,
she lurches splay-legged
and lands widdershins—
quite opposite
of where she means to be.

Her mother stands behind her,
looking down
        from her great height.
                Brown fuzz covers the calf—
                her mother has already
                licked her dry all over.

When I was born, my mother
said I was covered
in a fine black fuzz
*just like a little monkey.*

Now the giraffe mama
        leans down her long
                reticulated caramel and white
        neck,
        head-butts her calf—
she intends to help her stand—
        her knobby kneed baby,
        already six feet tall, who falls
        headfirst into a heap of
        leg angles and new hooves,

just as I did,
desperate, eighteen, damaged,
diving into marriage—

*that's what I should do, that's*

What is joy if not spindle-legged,
dark gray, with her mother's blaze,
flying around the corral, leaping
and swerving past me where I sit
watching, waiting for her to tire.

What is trust if not a tender creature
who trots over to you unbidden,
folds into your lap and sleeps.

Bareback and barefoot, a daisy chain
around her ankle, my mother smiles and poses
on the young Belgian, towhead toddler,
one of eight half-siblings, in her lap.

She's home on her day off from the latest
of the hired girl jobs
she's worked since eighth grade. "1938"
                    in the snapshot margin,
makes her seventeen.

The Belgian's chestnut coat and flax tail
shine in the black and white sunlight.
He's not more than two, won't reach
his full sixteen hands and 2,000 pounds
for two more years when he'll be
put to harness, his head through
the huge oval collar, check lines
threaded through hame rings,
traces hitched to the plow.

Full grown he'll be able to pull
8,000 pounds, but for now he's
standing still, head turned, ears pricked—

        my father three years down the road,
driving his green Packard, my father,
funny and tall, going into the grocery
business with my grandpa, my father
marrying the little Dane with the smile;
she'll never be hungry again, though she
won't ever believe that.

*Great Belgian, with your lineage*
*to medieval destrier chargers,*
*for this one day in the sunshine,*
*carry her, and the toddler, well.*

*What exactly happened?*
my friend asked.
So I told her.

A little pause, then,
*Well, what's the big deal?*
*I mean it's not as if*
*there was an actual rape or something*
*was there?*

No, not actual,
for actual he would have
actually have to have—
well, you know, don't you—
reader, must I tell you all of it too?

No, not actual, but something
and yes,
yes, I let him and yes, my friend,
yes, I let her too.

Covered in that black goop,
bedraggled and staggering
or flopping on the tar-ruined shore—
as if the disaster were a perverse
joke of a thousand cruel boys—
those Alaskan oil spill ducks,
white-winged divers, surf scoters,
the rescued ones, did it ever
all come off, were they ever
really clean again, or was it
never the same for them,
the great ocean of the world, the air?

When my mother had brain tumor surgery—
not to save her, but to relieve her—
they dug a crater exactly where
she kept her words. That was it.
When she woke up,
the rules had changed:
no more words from her.

Not another chance ever

for subtraction, no taking back
the scald of

*I wish you died that time you were so sick when you were little!*

No taking back, but no
possibility of repetition
either. A relief, wouldn't you think?

And her hands, don't suppose
she could write notes. Sparrows,
her hands became frantic sparrows diving
and diving at her gaunt belly
as if some cat were threatening
the already ruined nest of her.

No subtractions, no additions,
not a chance
for another hard stinging
slap across the face right before
she spat that death wish at me.

A relief, wouldn't you think?

But then, it also meant only once,
before they took her away
to put her under, we were talking
about the birthday party I threw
for Uncle Thomas. *Diane,* she said,
*you are a good person.*

You call up the tough kid
who wants to buy her,
have him come over, ride her
hard around the pasture,
let him jerk her mouth
this way, that way, hard,
the frantic yearling following
whinnying, wide-eyed. Then,
help load the both of them
into his sorry trailer; smack
her hard to get her in, a hard
enough whack to surprise her
up the rattling aluminum ramp;
never mind the long scrape
on her pastern, the trickle
of blood you glimpse as you
slam the tailgate shut; slam it hard,
you slam it sixty years shut.

My mother had this awful fear
of falling. When we all went
to the Grand Canyon, she sat
in the car and cried.

I didn't always know
she knew.
               Only once, before she died
she leaned over our Niagara,
dared to look down:

*That guy we bought your horse from,*
*he wasn't a very nice person, was he?*

No, he wasn't.

One little push
and over she would have gone.

Why didn't I?

For years, I dream
I am climbing up rock face when
I look up      in time to see
her coming down in a freefall—
Always, I stick out my arm
and catch her; that was my job. Then,
I hang onto the rock face
with one hand, her with the other.

Now, I live six hundred miles away
in Pennsylvania, the state
that gave us Jerry Sandusky
whose cover was football.

Actually, his cover wasn't the game
so much as one of its legendary heroes—
nothing sadder than a sullied legendary hero.

*Pedophile* is the clinical term,
the everyday word—*pervert*,
a noun, a verb, also an adjective—
so that those touched, sullied
are thus considered *perverted*.

Meanwhile, Jerry sits in prison
making his appeals: *bad lawyer,*
*should get a new trial,* he says,
*statute of limitations was up,* he says,
as if suffering had a shelf life.

Let me sing you
my son-in-law son:

Jack on his dawn drive
to work, to work in deep fog.
Jack saw them first. He stopped,
backed up, got out to take a look.
In field silence Jack stood
at the edge of the invisible,
at the electric fence, Jack
in dawn-gray cloud fog
saw the bay mare down,
saw the silver sack slip out,
saw a spindled foreleg poke
through its own warm pond—
Jack saw flattened feathers
of the filly unfold, saw her stand,
shiver, snuff the early air.
What I love is that Jack knew
to turn around, go back, quick get
wife and child; Jack knew
to drop the world hammer,
put his arm around Marie, hoist
sleepy Sarah to his shoulder,
whisper, *Look—over there.*

he showed up again last night
on Sunday morning relocated
to Pittsburgh in the warehouse district
as always we were alone
he had already parked
his rusting Chevy
dented humps of fenders and trunk
a giant blue crayfish
in bright sunlight he stood
between two empty brick buildings
same tight jeans ornate western belt
cinched under barrel chest same
worn flannel shirt gray-blue eyes
same straw-colored hair
*what do you want* I whispered
he said nothing and raised his hand
which wasn't a hand but a hook
a chrome hook that caught the sun
as he twisted it like a laser
in my eyes    I backed up
*what do you want* I whispered
he said nothing but smiled working
and working the blinding light
coming toward me again

I have allowed myself
no other horses, no riding.

She who meant beauty,
who meant love, who meant pain,

a bay like her,
driving today, I spotted her
at the far end of a pasture—
dark burnished copper
shining in sunlight, black
mane and tail, just like her—

I've gone back there,
stared at the long meadow
morphed into suburb,
McMansions sprung up
all along the little stream.

On the hill, the red barn
a gentrified beige and teal.
No sign of the girl I was;
she's already dismounted,
slid back the heavy door,
gone inside.

Let what will happen, happen.
Let her love the horses.
Let her adore the man.
Then, let her not hoard
the wrongdoing visited
upon her, let it no longer
cower within her.

Why this? Why now?

Say it's the moon
at its September perigee,
close as it will ever be
before it subsides
back to farthest February.

Say the moon rises now, huge,
blood-orange, refusing
to be ignored, say it's time
to gather and reap even
the commonest of harvests,
say it's time to winnow.

He's safe now, dead somewhere
far away from me. And my parents,
they're safe too, below deck
in their bunks with the lids on
out there in Wisconsin where
all's calm down in the earthen sea.

Up above, their headstones line up,
two front teeth in a grassy mouth.
They haven't got anything
to say for themselves. Sometimes,
I'd sink him there too, massacre
them all together, leave them
to deal with each other sunk
in Holy Innocents Cemetery
where nobody needs a thing.

Other times, I'd gather them
gently from the grave, put each
in a separate wooden boat
or a frail Moses basket of pitch
and wattle. Then I'd send
all three of them off down
quieter, kinder streams,
to the same endless ocean.

# NOTES

The first epigraph is from Czesław Miłosz's poem "Annalena" in *Czeslaw Milosz New and Collected, 1931–2001* (New York: HarperCollins, 1988).

The second epigraph is from the introduction to D. A. Powell's collection *Tea* (Middletown, CT: Wesleyan, 1998).

Much of the information about the moon in *Perigee* is from www.moonconnection.com.

The poem segment beginning "What I had to say on the occasion of Roy Moore's defeat" refers to a US Senate special election held in December 2017 in which former Alabama Chief Justice and District Attorney Roy Moore was a candidate. Before the election, several women made allegations of sexual misconduct against Moore. Two of Moore's accusers were underage at the time of the alleged misconduct, one fourteen, another fifteen; the age of consent in Alabama is sixteen. Many prominent US Senate Republicans called for Moore to drop out of the Senate race. President Donald Trump continued to endorse Moore, who lost the election. Moore often appeared at political rallies riding his tall pinto horse.

The poem segment beginning "It was nighttime and Father was driving" is indebted to Elizabeth Bishop's poem "In the Waiting Room" from *The Complete Poems, 1927–1979* (New York: Noonday Press; Farrar, Straus, and Giroux, 1979).

The poem segment beginning "When Christine Blasey Ford" refers to a 2018 US Senate Judiciary Committee hearing, broadcast live, regarding the nomination of then US Supreme Court nominee Brett Kavanaugh. Blasey Ford, a Stanford University research psychologist, made an allegation of sexual assault against Kavanaugh, stating that the assault took place when both were teenagers and describing the alleged assault in detail at the hearing. Kavanaugh's nomination was confirmed by the Senate.

The quote in the segment beginning "Tess's long tale of love" is from Thomas Hardy's novel *Tess of the d'Urbervilles* (London: Macmillan Collector's Library, 2018).

The poem segment beginning "Now, I live six hundred miles away" references the Penn State child sex abuse scandal which became public in 2011. Jerry Sandusky, a retired assistant football coach, who continued to have access to Penn State athletic facilities after his retirement, was convicted of forty-five counts of child sexual abuse, much of which occurred with young children and adolescents on the Penn State campus over a period of at least fifteen years. An independent investigation commissioned by the Penn State Board of Trustees concluded that legendary head coach Joe Paterno as well as the university's president, vice-president, and athletic director were aware of the abuse as early as 1998 and had engaged in a cover-up. Paterno died shortly thereafter. In the criminal case that followed, the school administrators pleaded or were found guilty of child endangerment and were sentenced to jail terms, fines, and probation in 2017. Sandusky was sentenced to a minimum of thirty years in prison. He remains in prison as of this writing and continues to maintain his innocence.

# ACKNOWLEDGMENTS

Grateful acknowledgment is given to the publications in which the following poem segments first appeared, sometimes in earlier versions:

*Poetry East*: "Let me sing you"

*South Dakota Review*: "Dawn in Jutland: gulls lift a flock of white commas"

*Voices from the Attic Anthology*, Vol. 22: "When my Mother had brain surgery"

*What Rough Beast*: "What I had to say on the occasion of Roy Moore's defeat:"

*Zone 3*: "Someone's planted perennials along Ohio 71"

Many people over many years helped me to write and publish this book. Thanks to:

Natasha Trethewey for choosing to honor this book with the Brittingham Prize.

Everyone at the University of Wisconsin Press for bringing the book into being, especially Ron Wallace for his belief in this work.

John L. Meyer, my first extraordinary poetry teacher.

Judith Vollmer, my most recent extraordinary teacher.

My wonderful teachers in the Warren Wilson Program for Writers: the late Steve Orlen, the late Tony Hoagland, Michael Ryan, and Ellen Bryant Voigt.

The Warren Wilson Alumni Conference where I presented an early version of this work for manuscript review.

Hedgebrook for the gift of time, beauty, and "radical hospitality" while I worked on these poems.

Ruth Hendricks for the gift of an author photo.

Richard St. John for the gift of friendship and for reading an early chapbook version of this work.

The community of the Madwomen in the Attic Creative Writing Program at Carlow University, especially Jan Beatty, fearless leader and inspiration.

Joy Katz and Celeste Gainey for professional help and personal consolation.

M. J. Place and Carolyn Luck for the gift of enduring friendship and belief in my work.

My children, who taught me what it is to love a child.

Jon Spiegel, who defended the girl I was, for years, until I could too.

My husband, John McCall, holy man and rock.

The poem segment beginning "You call up the tough kid" is for Jan Beatty.

The poem segment beginning "It was nighttime and Father was driving" is for Ellen Bryant Voigt.

The poem segment beginning "My father reclines" is for Judith Vollmer.